Forever Speaking

CAROLYN A. STOVALL

ISBN: 979-8-88945-463-2

eISBN: 979-8-88945-464-9

Brilliant Books Literary

137 Forest Park Lane Thomasville

North Carolina 27360 USA

Printed in the United States of America

To God who inspired me to write.

Acknowledgments

Thanks to family and friends for their encouragement
May God continued blessing be upon you.
To the readers of "Forever Speaking"
May this book have a life changing
effect within your lives.

Contents

Godly Surprise

A new beginning is on the rise
I Standup straight for a godly surprise
Beloved always surely, you're the one
Search many years from heaven
Son sent on earth
My kingdom comes
Unity in one

Butterfly

Flapping wings colorful dreams
Temporary glory manifests my story
Imagine yourself as a beautiful butterfly
Of freedom

Intimacy

Deny self away
Spend time kneel down to pray
Communed with me in my glory
Where answers are revealed
Created ideals
No one else hears
Just between us two
Unknown mysteries release
Through you

Spoken

Songs written from heaven
Spoken words connecting together
Reaching high to the sky
with no limits
Speaking into existence
Coming to life
Creating the world
In my surrounding presence
Were syllables echo's straight from heaven

Dancing

Dancing with Jesus
Dressed in white
Long robe fits just right
Dancing with Jesus
All through the night
Angels surround me
Smiling rejoicing
In his arms as he holds me tight
Taken two steps to the left
Two steps to the right
Time spent basting in glory
He's my everything my helpmate
That's the whole story
Dancing with Jesus
Oh
What a wonderful sight …

Judah Praise

Six o'clock Saturday morning Church
doors open for the people of praise
Clapping hands
In the spirit so high
Speaking tongues
Judah praise
Judah praise
The promise of amazed
Judah praise

Second Chance

A second chance is the best
the Third fourth or fifth test
Become stronger determined equipped ready
Loaded down with precious stones
Of god's greatest gifts
Perseverance pushing you near
Because I'm called here
Place of destiny
Before formed in a mother's womb
The enemy knows but can't stop the moved
Going forward not looking back
Setting eyes on the creator
For my second chance fight.....

God Has Me

Between two big trees
Living without no reason of need
This place is safe
This place is cool
"I know God has me"
In the palms of his hand
Loving caring
Making a plan
God has me
Raising me up to become a great man
To speak to millions about his salvation plan
God has me ......

Birthing

Spiritual connection
For intercession
Wailing weeping women
Crying out pain
Bringing forth child
A Spiritual reign
Purpose came out
Early morning midnight hour
Positioning for god's birthing power…..

Unity

We are One
but out of placed
with different voices
languages of hate
A called to unity
We must face
Every day pray for unity
God's way ………

…..how wonderful and pleasant for god's people to dwell together in unity.

Psalm 133:1

Breakthrough

Yesterday in the park
Up and down the trails
My meditation starts
Words I once heard
Came flowing back to me
Remembering god's promises
That set people free
Powerfully spoken
Successfully broken
By a breakthrough walk in the park......

........the law he meditates day and night.

Psalm 1:2

Wandering Eyes

Wandering eyes admired on fire
Burning flames that never ends
Eternity my friend
Choose life of peace joy contents
Wandering eyes
Stop wandering to see
If when or what will be .....

Decisions

It's raining outside
Contemplating what to do
About the decisions I made
One year ago
I thought I needed out of the blue
Should I or should I not
I haven't come this far to give up now
A little voice whisper to me
Looking at the circumstances will
Frighten anybody away
What's in front of you can easily
Disappear today
Now the rain has stopped
But life still goes on
So don't let past mistakes keep you from moving on
Learn from them
That's what makes you strong.......

Hidden

Sleeping in the park
Covered by newspaper from head to knee
Reading the good book of Genesis
Where God create earth from sea to sea
And after six days
He rested and blessed
Which made special for me
Created man from dust in his sleep
Then woman came along for company
Placed in the garden midst of thee
When eaten wrong fruit
Tricked by the enemy Covered by shame
Lost and afraid
Nakedness blame
Knowledge between good and bad
God's spoken word came to passed......

.......in the beginning god created the earth and sky.

Genesis 1:1

Cave

in a cave experience
Hungry unable to eat
Thirsty can't seem to drink
As I Cry to sleep
But God was there
In a place nobody knows unaware
Just me and him
Negative thoughts flows that I dread
Confused about being dead
What's the truth? I said
But god was there
In a cave experience
Alone and surrounded by people
Speaking Jeremiah
No one will listen
I'm coming out in due time
Because god was there
And I will be fine……

Pastor's Heart

Chosen by god
Not by man
A piece of him within hand
Compassion bundled with grace
Saving mercy faith
More than selfish hate
Hearing obeying the voice above
Feeding sheep with knowledge
Understanding meets all love.......

Fight

Holding on for dear life
I fight
I will not give up
Every breath I take
Every teardrop I make
Against the enemy who's
Trying to take me away
I fight
Oh dear lord
You say to live and not die
So I fight………

.......I shall not die but live and declare the words of the lord.

Psalm 118:17

Everlasting

This old shell no longer dragging me down
Spirit freedom heaven bound
To my earthy mom and dad
I graciously thank you for good times and sad
My love for you will never change
Now I return to the heavenly father from which I came
Where there's no more sickness
No disease or stickling needles fearing me
I am free, free as I be
Go tell others about Jesus plan
To give their heart just as me ....

.....whoever believes in him should not perish but have everlasting life.

John 3:16

Stripping

Stripping me just as Job
What sin have I done
What sin have I sowed
Did I disobey
Did I not pray
Stripping me of all I have
Bent over fetal position
Waiting to die
No of course
That's a lie
Stripping to be restored
And Live better than before……..

Something for Jesus

Doing something for Jesus is simply through me
Doing something for Jesus a smile a kiss on the cheek
When morning comes the sun shines bright
Showing reflection, the Jesus in you
Walking in boldness
Confessing his word from me to you Book of instructions
created for thee
As God spoke his prophets wrote
They heard many will see
A voice from their heart
Dreams visions may appear
Follow me as I follow him the lamb of God
Seeing Jesus crystal clear
The way out is through me
Redemption paid with a price confessing lord Jesus Christ
Now saved as disciples do what you're called
Doing something for Jesus is spreading love to all.......

Morning

Morning walks talks for cure
A pathway healing for sure
Digestive tract spine problems
The enemy tries to attack
Disconnect what god made perfect
Is no longer the fact
Walking in victory
Talking by faith
Life speaks louder
Divine healing takes place
Movement in motions starts a brand-new day
A new life is on the way.........

My Flower

You're a flower blossoming each and every hour
Day by day
Minute by minute
As the sun completes to finish
Open up and let go
My little flower
To show ....

Snow

A knock at the door
"who is it ?" I ask
My son opens
Its snow fallen in the night
Snowdrops hits my feet
Tickles as I sleep
A presence awakens me
In a dream god spoke
Snow is my word I placed at your feet
I am preparing you to speak to millions
The gospel has to be preached
Chosen vessel far away you'll go
Covered anointing
Taken places where my glory is hungry to come........

Needs

Rejoicing in the lord
Making melody of song
We are created to worship all day long
Birds of the air
Birds with no worries
Birds with no care
God knows their needs
God has answers for every human being
Look to him
Do not fear
A setting example is birds and their needs.......

.......the birds do not plant seeds or gather harvest yet god provides for them

Matthews 6:26

Touch

By touching the word
It will make you free
Healing the body
Healing the mind
Healing the soul
Of past bad memories
Released by faith for good in thee
"woman who touches the hem"
Touches the word in me……….

.......she touch the edge of his cloak and instantly her bleeding stopped

Luke 8:44

Jerusalem Wall

Coming to the Jerusalem wall to pray
I kneel down
Bowing or stand up straight
Moved my body from side to side
The back-and-forth way
Pacing the grounds at the Jerusalem wall
I'm coming back for my beloved place
Other nations
Please take notice
Follow the Jerusalem way
More times a day to pray…………….

..............pray for the peace of Jerusalem that you will have peace and safety within your walls

Psalm 122:6-7

Unforgiveness

A mind running
With thoughts of fear
Anxiety of people who lied
And tried to crucify
My world turned upside down
Focus on what offend
Unforgiveness will kill steal destroy
That's the devil revenge
Letting go to healed
Jesus thirty nine stripes for what made right
He died on the cross
After three days and night
He rose again for forgiveness.........

.........be kind and forgiving to one another as god has forgiven you

Ephesians 4:32

Encourage

Missing church something hard
A famine land
A broken heart
Encourage yourself
As king David dance
Let us gather together
On one accord
Singing worshiping praising
Glory to god
Our souls are covered by pastor in charge
Receiving Jesus at heart
Encourage yourself for a life change start.......

Little children

Where can you be
Somewhere hiding near
Somewhere hiding far
At any given moment
Spiritually you are
Angelic angels was are
Little children playing
Little children protecting
Little children proclaiming
God uses us
As he sits on his throne
Giving our orders forever
"he shall give his angels charge over thee"
As he said in the book of Matthew 4:6
You see...........

Now act like it

To hear from the father
To hear him not
To hear the father
To not missed the mark
Obey what he says
Praise god Praise
Now act like it
As the preacher said to a few
Surrounding the altar for all to view
Watching the prophet prophesy
Deeper you are
Louder you hear
Ignoring me because of fear
Humility comes before honor
Hearing the father in obedience
Course correction for a lesson learned
Now act like it........................

Here

As I lay in bed
Teardrops fall down my cheeks
A vision at night
As I sleep
God's presence awakens me
He's here
He's everywhere surrounding me
I need thee
Worshiping
As I lay there in bed
Thirsting to be near
Just as he to me
The more I reach
The farther he be
As a deer pants for water
"My child" he says to me
I am here always here with thee.....................

… thirst for you Oh Lord just as a deer for cool water.

Psalm 42:1

Represent

A coat of many colors
Talents and gifts of no other
"wear then Joseph"
In spite of the naysayers
You're favored
You're Anointed for the task
Represent god's first
Brotherly love that lasts.............

..........his father made him a coat of many colors.

Genesis 37:3

John

A man name John
With a Shinning face glowing beyond
In a small room chapel place
He just appeared
Reading his bible
Fascinated by truth
Ask for prayer
God is always there
Have a nice day
An angel before noon
John in the flesh
Maybe he came to spread the good news.............

Vision

Vision at work
Designed for us
Without vision
I may perish to dust
Fading away too soon
Grasp your vision
Hold on tight
Don't let it out of sight
Don't look back
Don't delay
For my people awaits
For a vision that works………………………..

. . . write the vision and make it plain

Habakkuk 2:2

Salvation

This is a free gift from God above
From me to thee with unconditional love
Lift up your hands and repeat after me
I received Jesus as my savior and friend
I welcome him into my heart to love again
I repent of all my sins
As you cleanse me from within
Now I am saved
I can share with others and not be afraid
God sent Jesus to die on a cross
Suffer and bleed for everyone lost
Come to me and receive my agape love
You are all god's children by the shedding of the blood
Jesus, his son..............

.........received and believe in god ,therefore you are children of god

John 1:12